TO: _____

FROM: _____

Other books by Gregory E. Lang:

Because You Are My Son...

WHAT I HOPE YOU NEVER FORGET

GREGORY E. LANG

CUMBERLAND HOUSE™

Published by Cumberland House Publishing, an imprint of Sourcebooks, Inc.
P.O. Box 4410, Naperville, Illinois 60567-4410
(630) 961-3900
Fax: (630) 961-2168
www.sourcebooks.com

Printed and bound in the United States of America
LB 10 9 8 7 6 5 4 3 2 1

To Mom and Dad and all those blessed with sons.

Place a personal photograph here.

Include a personal note here.

INTRODUCTION

I wrote my first book, *Why a Daughter Needs a Dad*, nearly a dozen years ago. It was originally a letter to who was then my only child, reassuring her of my love and commitment to being the best dad I could possibly be. In that book I shared my hopes and dreams about what her future might hold and what role I would play in that future.

During the ensuing years I have reflected on that book and wondered about how well I've lived up to the expectations I created when I put my thoughts and feelings on paper. I think I've done rather well on many measures, but I also must admit to having failed on numerous others. Indeed, there has been joy and disappointment in my home. I've made as many child-rearing mistakes as any parent and often find myself envious of other parents who I believe handled a certain situation or dilemma far better than I did or might have.

Yet in spite of my parenting missteps I continue to desire as much as anything else to be the best parent I can possibly be. As any parent knows, the happiness and well-being of your own child is the highest achievement you can hope for. No matter how often we may blunder as parents, or how often we face disappointments, nothing quenches our love for our children, extinguishes our desire to see them thrive and prosper, or thwarts our ambition to have a meaningful role in their lives.

That is why we parents do what we do: save baby teeth and locks of hair, tempera-paint masterpieces and yellowed report cards; attend every recital, spelling bee, and sporting event we can cram into our schedules; wait sleeplessly for teens to come home; fall asleep praying for wisdom and miracles; cry at high school graduations; and do everything we can to postpone our children's eventual departure from home. Because it is our children who give us something that cannot be obtained from any other source—a sense of place in a life that is more important than your own, the life of your child.

And now all these years later, years of saving, watching, waiting, and praying, I still have high hopes and big dreams for the children in my home. I am not unique on that aspect of parenting, I'm sure. But one aspect of my parenting is different from the experience of many other parents: I do not have a son.

I've wondered what my life might have been like if I had also had a hand in raising a boy. When I've written about parent-son relationships it has always been from my perspective as a son, never as a parent of a son. When I've wanted to put myself in the shoes of a father of a son, I've thought of my dad and his relationships with his four sons, or my male cousins and their sons. Yet I know that this exercise has its limits. I've never taught a boy how to throw a football, catch a fish, start a lawn mower, or to be a gentleman.

Until now.

I've recently been blessed with the companionship and admiration of a twelve-year-old boy named Cameron. I am his mentor and he is my young friend. With him I'm experiencing a few things that are quite new to me. We watch movies with more explosions than dialogue; discuss cars, technology, and girls (in that order); repair bicycles; work in the yard; and yes, I'm schooling him in the ways of chivalry.

I'm loving our time together; he's giving me something my life might have otherwise gone without—the pleasure and challenge of helping to raise a boy into a man. And as is the case with my girls, I want nothing more than to bring my best to that effort.

I want him to be happy, do well, go far, and to remember me.

So in the end then, this book is really for Cameron. Although he is not my son, he is in my heart and prayers, and my hope for him abounds.

May your father and mother always be glad,
and may you always give them reason to rejoice.

Because
You Are
My Son...

*Because you are
my son...*

I've loved you from the moment

our eyes first met.

The most handsome face

in the world has always been yours.

You may not remember everything,

but

because you are my son,

I remember it all:

your heartwarming laughter,

your big smile first thing in the morning,

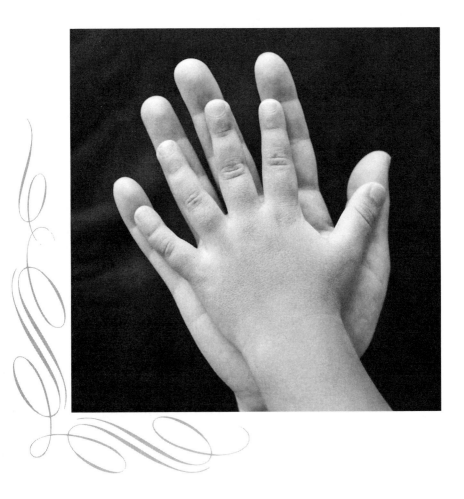

your tight hugs whenever I reached for you.

Your tiny hand in mine.

The sound of your little feet

running across the floor.

Those afternoons when you rode

on my shoulders,

and the first time you called out my name.

You are my son, brimming with adventure.

You introduced a little rough-and-tumble

into my life.

We rolled around in the grass for hours

and screamed on the swing when

our feet were above our heads.

We built castles in the sandbox

and rode our bikes around the block

over and over again.

At night we chased fireflies in the backyard

and then read from your favorite books

until you fell asleep.

I still think of all those mornings we shared

chocolate chip pancakes for breakfast.

You are my son...

alongside you I rediscovered

how to play and have fun.

You reminded me to use my imagination

and helped me to believe in comic book heroes

and superpowers once more.

You've brought more laughter into my life

as I've watched you grow up.

We learned together when you

turned to me for help

and asked me all those tough,

but necessary, questions.

I loved caring for your cuts and bruises

and being the one who taught you

what you needed to know.

You leaned on me when you faced

your first challenges,

and you delighted me when you found

your own strengths.

You filled my life with that special something

I'd been missing,

and you have enriched my life in more ways

than I can count.

You are my son...

and when you found your place

in the world, I found mine:

being the parent you needed.

I've loved that mischievous smile on your face

and your bold and carefree ways.

I've loved watching you chart

your own journey

and being your compass

whenever you were lost.

You've added immeasurable joy to my life.

You've indulged me when

I wanted to hug you forever,

you always soaked in the love

I had to give you,

and you gave me your love and

respect without hesitation.

You are my son,

you are my heart.

You've made me feel as if

I'm the luckiest parent in the world.

Watching you become a young man

has been a blessing to me,

and no matter how much

you've grown and changed,

our deep bond has remained

strong and true.

You have been an endless source of

understanding and encouragement,

and you never hesitate to help me when

I call out for you.

Because you are my son,

you remind me to slow down, relax,

and enjoy the day with you.

You've been forgiving when

I was frustrated and impatient.

You always seem to cheer me up when I'm blue,

and you remind me not to take

myself so seriously.

You keep me in a peaceful state of mind.

Through your eyes I've come to

see the world differently;

I worry much less and laugh much more.

We bring out the best in each other,

and sometimes I can see a little bit of me in you.

We both like anchovies on our pizza,

and extra cheese on our big juicy burgers.

We can chat for hours and never get bored,

and sometimes we just sit,

say nothing at all, and

are happy together nonetheless.

Yet in ways we are different from one another,

and those differences can frustrate us both.

But our frustrations are never permanent.

Nothing can come between us.

Because you are my son,

my belief in you never fades,

and you are always first in my prayers.

I'm thrilled with each of your accomplishments

and am never disappointed in your best efforts.

The love between us continues to grow,

and although the years have changed us,

our relationship remains

as strong as ever.

Even as life has taken us our separate ways,

you've shown you rely on me still.

When I miss you I look through

all the father's day presents

you've given me and

the treasures I've saved.

Each one reminds me that

I'll always have a part of you with me.

We love the comfort of togetherness,

yet respect each other's private time and space.

You don't mind when I call to say "I miss you,"

and now and then you call me to say that too.

No matter where our separate paths take us,

we always come together again.

———————

You still manage to laugh at my tired, old jokes,

and I'm always eager to hear about

your exciting new day.

You never have so much to do that you can't

stop to spend a little time with me,

and you remind me I'm never too old to wrestle

like we once used to.

I'm so proud of who you've become,

and I'm so hopeful about where you are going.

Wherever you end up, one thing will be sure—

I'll be proud of you there and then too.

You have shared your heart and

your dreams with me,

and your dreams have become mine.

Because you are my son,

in my heart and dreams you will always be.

ACKNOWLEDGMENTS

Thank you, God, for without your blessing my writings would still be in a shoe box in the dark recesses of my closet. My words are yours; I am merely the hand that puts them on paper. To you goes the Glory!

Behind every good book is a great team, and that is certainly the case with this book. I have also been blessed with the love and support, creative inspiration, and good old-fashioned dogged determination of many people who have guided my writing through the transition from words scrawled on paper to a hardback book on a bookstore shelf. With that truth in mind, I'd like to give a heartfelt thanks to the following people:

My dear wife, Jill, who encourages me more than anyone, who has unabashed faith in my person, and who doesn't scold me too harshly as she redlines every spelling, grammar, and structural error in my rough drafts. She contributes far more to my success than she gets credit for. I love her beyond measure; she is my best friend.

The young daughters in my life, Meagan Lang and Linley Davis. Without their love, affection, and kind indulgence of my sometimes unpleasant behavior as deadlines approach, this book could not have been written. I'd also like to thank Cameron, the young boy I mentor, for giving me something to do other than pay for another pedicure in between writing projects.

All my new friends at Sourcebooks, Inc., who did a stellar job turning my vague idea into this book. In particular, I'd like to thank Dominique Raccah who believed in my talent and chose to give me a new platform for expressing myself, Peter Lynch for advocating for me, and Sara Kase, my editor, for bringing my vision to a beautiful reality. I'm so pleased to be in a new publishing home and look forward to our mutually rewarding future.

My family, friends, neighbors, and even a few strangers who remained patient with me as I posed, reposed, and posed them again in a vain effort to capture the perfect photographs to illustrate this book. I thank you all for being the faces to accompany these words.

And finally I wish to thank my parents, Gene and Dianne Lang, who have been my best teachers of all things about parenting during the last fifty years. Thinking about how they managed to do so much for their five children over all these years still drops my jaw.

To Contact the Author

Write in care of the publisher:
Gregory E. Lang
c/o Sourcebooks, Inc.
P. O. Box 4410
Naperville, IL 60567-4410

Email the author or visit his website:
gregoryelang@gmail.com
www.gregoryelang.com